W9-CZR-477

GERMS
DISEASE-CAUSING ORGANISMS™

VIRUSES

MARGAUX BAUM and NATALIE GOLDSTEIN

rosen publishing's
rosen central®

Published in 2017 by The Rosen Publishing Group, Inc.
29 East 21st Street, New York, NY 10010

First Edition

Library of Congress Cataloging-in-Publication Data
Names: Baum, Margaux, author. | Goldstein, Natalie, author.
Title: Viruses / Margaux Baum and Natalie Goldstein.
Description: First edition. | New York : Rosen Central, 2017. | Series:
 Germs: disease causing organisms | Audience: Grades 5-8. | Includes
 bibliographical references and index.
Identifiers: LCCN 2016002013| ISBN 9781477788578 (library bound) | ISBN
 9781477788554 (pbk.) | ISBN 9781477788561 (6-pack)
Subjects: LCSH: Viruses--Juvenile literature.
Classification: LCC QR365 .G65 2017 | DDC 579.2--dc23
LC record available at http://lccn.loc.gov/2016002013

Manufactured in China

CONTENTS

INTRODUCTION

If you were paying attention to the news in early October 2014, it seemed there was wall-to-wall coverage of a new and deadly threat to the public health of Americans. The Centers for Disease Control and Prevention (CDC), the U.S. government agency in charge of tracking, preventing, and helping treat disease, announced that Thomas Eric Duncan, a native of the West African nation of Liberia, was the first known U.S.-based victim of the deadly Ebola infection.

Visiting relatives in Dallas, Texas, Duncan fell ill at the end of September 2014 and was hospitalized. He had not displayed symptoms until five days after his arrival in the United States. American hospitals were not quite prepared for the Ebola outbreak, including the strict guidelines for keeping the infection from spreading from patients they were treating. Two of Duncan's caregivers were diagnosed, and one, a nurse, even flew to Cleveland, Ohio, and back to Texas before she developed symptoms.

The CDC and other government agencies went into overdrive, trying to figure out where the disease may have already spread. Only one other victim was identified: Dr. Craig Spencer. He was a physician helping treat Ebola patients in Guinea, and he had also recently flown in from West Africa. He was a New York resident, and officials tried to retrace his steps—he had taken the train and gone bowling one evening—to try to warn those who had possibly been exposed.

The Ebola epidemic barely touched the United States, and the only fatality was Liberian national Thomas Eric Duncan.

But the fear of this viral infection consumed the public's attention for weeks. Unfortunately, the extent of the damage Ebola would do was far greater overseas. For some time before the U.S. cases, and through late 2015, Ebola had claimed many victims, mainly in West Africa, killing more than 11,000 people.

Ebola is one of the more fearsome examples of a type of organism that causes ill health in human beings: the virus. Viruses are behind the numerous types of influenza, or flu, that afflict people all over the world. Other relatively common sicknesses—such as children getting chickenpox, or sexually active people getting sexually transmitted diseases or infections (STDs, or STIs)—also arise due to viruses. More dangerous and debilitating conditions also arise from viruses. Acquired immunodeficiency syndrome (AIDS) is caused when victims catch the human immunodeficiency virus (HIV).

Viruses are specialized in their construction—they can multiply only within the living cells of other organisms. They infect humans, animals, plants, and even other microorganisms, such as bacteria. In this resource, we will investigate how they work, how to avoid them, and how they are treated and controlled.

CHAPTER 1

THE HUMAN BODY AND VIRUSES

Viruses can be considered the ultimate parasites. They can do nothing on their own and instead depend on other living beings, whose cells they invade. Inside, they manipulate their hosts and force them to manufacture copies of the virus. Because they do not carry out their own life processes, they are not considered cells, but something else altogether. These tiny bits of genetic material wrapped in a protective coat of protein—a single one is just a millionth of an inch long—are so small that they can invade other microorganisms, such as bacteria. They force cells to reproduce their genetic material. In many cases, they can overwhelm and completely break down the host organisms they infect.

Genes consist of strands of deoxyribonucleic acid, also known as DNA. When a cell divides, its DNA is replicated, and one copy goes to each daughter cell. Another genetic substance, ribonucleic acid, or RNA, is crucial in carrying out DNA's instructions for making vital cell proteins. Some viruses contain DNA; others contain RNA. A virus attaches itself to the surface of a host cell.

Cells are selective about which chemicals they let in or keep out. Special receptors on a cell's surface permit entry only to those chemicals the cell needs. A receptor is like a lock. The needed chemical is like the key that unlocks the receptor. Viruses mimic the keys that fit the receptors on the type of cell they seek to infect. After attaching to the receptor, the virus either enters the cell or injects its genetic material into it. The virus uses the host cell's proteins and enzymes to replicate viral genes and build new viral particles. These new viruses leave the cell and spread to a new host.

Some viruses spread through the air. As everyone knows, cold viruses are spread by coughing and sneezing. Other viruses spread through contaminated food or water, from mother to child in the womb or in mother's milk, from biting insects, or from contact with infected people.

LINES OF DEFENSE: THE IMMUNE SYSTEM

The human body's immune system recognizes and destroys alien invaders such as viruses. Circulating in the blood, immune system cells come into contact with other cells. Each cell displays on its surface a sample of whatever material is being produced inside it. Immune cells can distinguish between acceptable cell materials and foreign substances that don't belong. When immune cells encounter viruses or viral proteins, they destroy them.

VIRUSES

The immune system's first line of defense is the skin. The outer skin has layers of dead cells. Viruses infect only living cells. Unless it is cut, skin presents an impenetrable barrier to viruses. Even "inner" skin, the cells lining the mucous membranes of the mouth, nose, and eyes, can block or destroy many germs.

If a virus does get through, the next line of defense includes the leukocytes, or white blood cells, of which there are more than a dozen types. Cells such as phagocytes and macrophages work like the body's garbage collectors and consume viruses and debris from dead cells.

White blood cells known as B cells also produce antibodies, chemicals that can bind to viruses and their antigens, the toxins they produce, and prevent their entry. These antibodies work together with about twenty different proteins produced in the liver that can kill viruses as part of the body's complement system. If these proteins fail to kill the viruses, they bind to them. Like warning flags, they signal infection to other immune cells that can kill the viruses.

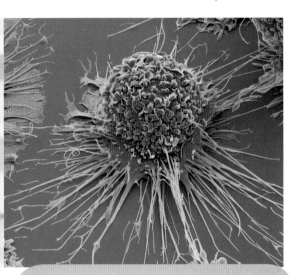

A scanning electron micrograph (SEM) captures a macrophage that has been activated in the human body. Its job is to engulf and ingest any foreign entities and substances that may threaten the body.

Interferon is one such "alarm protein" crucial to the complement system. Infected cells usually produce huge amounts of RNA, which triggers interferon production in the cell. As its name suggests, interferon "interferes" with viral replication in infected cells. Interferon also binds to other cells and induces them to commit suicide. Excess cell death, caused either by interferon or by viruses, activates other immune responses. Full-scale attack by the immune system causes inflammation. This results when some white blood cells release histamine, dilating blood vessels and bringing more blood and white blood cells to the site of infection.

This molecular model shows what a gamma interferon protein looks like. These proteins are released by infected cells to inform nearby cells of germs.

VIRUSES

WHERE DID VIRUSES COME FROM?

Nobody knows for sure where viruses came from. Some scientists speculate that these particles of genetic material broke away from animal and plant genes and found a way to exist independently.

DNA contains "jumping genes," snippets of DNA that can detach from one part of a DNA strand and reattach at another site. Some jumping genes contain instructions for making useful proteins. It's believed that some of these gene segments found a way to leave their "home" cells and exist parasitically.

In early Earth history, these genes may have moved from one organism to another organism, increasing genetic diversity and aiding evolution. Now they exist independently, but they need hosts to reproduce.

Sometimes, a virus will invade the body and reproduce so quickly that it overwhelms the ability of antibodies and proteins to fight it. Then the body brings out its big guns—the killer T cells. T cells have surface receptors that contain random segments of proteins, so they're extremely diverse. A T cell recognizes and destroys only those viruses whose proteins match its own.

Despite this impressive armory, the immune system sometimes has trouble fighting viral infections. Many viruses can go about their business inside cells undetected at first. Often, it is not until a lot of interferon is produced by infected cells or until many cells have died that immune responses are activated. Viruses also use a variety of ingenious strategies to outwit the immune system or at least to hold it off long enough to allow them to reproduce and spread.

CHAPTER 2

VIRAL DISEASES

Pick some of the more common sicknesses out there; viruses are behind many of them. For instance, there are 150 types of rhinovirus alone that can cause the common cold. It is so common partly because the virus spreads in air droplets when an infected person coughs or sneezes. Rhinoviruses affect the nose, mouth, and upper respiratory airways because they are more exposed and relatively cool than other parts of the body.

Rhinoviruses contain a single strand of RNA. After binding to a cell surface, a rhinovirus injects its genetic material into the cell cytoplasm. The virus's genetic material contains one protein that causes the cell to begin copying viral RNA. The cell is forced to make numerous copies of the virus's RNA very quickly. Each new virus is then enclosed in a protein coat. The newly created viruses burst out of the cell, killing it. Within days after infection, phagocytes and natural killer cells destroy the virus, and the cold passes.

THE INFLUENZA VIRUS AND THE FLU

There are three types of influenza virus: A, B, and C. Influenza A is the deadliest and also the most "devious." Influenza A targets respiratory cells. The virus has a surface protein that matches "receptor" proteins on the respiratory cells. The protein attaches to the receptor and coats itself with some cell membrane, then enters the cell. Once inside, the virus sheds its protective coat and releases its genes—short segments of single-stranded RNA—into the cytoplasm. The RNA moves into the cell nucleus, where viral gene replication occurs.

Influenza A carries an enzyme called polymerase, which switches an infected cell from its resting mode to its reproducing mode and makes it replicate viral RNA. Polymerase replicates viral RNA efficiently but not very precisely. Many mistakes are made in copying the viral RNA—these are called mutations. Influenza A's RNA replication is so prone to error that many of the replicated viruses are mutants. Influenza A is so successful because its genes are constantly changing; the immune system can hardly keep up.

Just hours after the initial infection, thousands of new viruses are created in the respiratory cells.

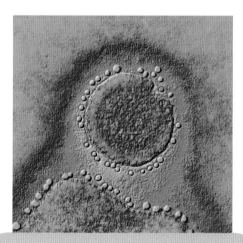

This colored transmission electron micrograph (TEM) image shows a close-up of the avian influenza virus (avian flu), of the strain H7N9, which first emerged in China in March 2013 and then spread internationally.

This should trigger production of enormous quantities of interferon and activate the immune system. However, influenza A has a protein that partially disables interferon production in infected cells. This buys influenza time to reproduce and spread. Eventually, though, the death of so many respiratory cells triggers an immune response. The infected person develops antibodies against influenza A. However, the virus mutates so often that the immune system's defense against one strain is useless against mutant strains. This is why the flu is longer lasting and more serious than the common cold.

THE MEASLES VIRUS

The measles virus also spreads through the air. This virus can infect the whole body because it has a surface protein that can connect to receptors on most body cells. The measles virus contains a single strand of RNA. The measles virus's surface proteins bind to cell receptors, and the virus's RNA is injected into the cytoplasm. Measles also carries its own polymerase to get the cell to replicate viral RNA in the cytoplasm. New measles viruses bud from the infected cell and are carried in the blood to uninfected cells.

Curiously, another reason that measles successfully infects the whole body is because it allows macrophages to kill it during its initial symptomless invasion of the lungs. As these viruses are killed, immune system cells carry samples of viral proteins to the lymph nodes. But the virus has actually infected these cells. The infected cells pass on the viral proteins to other immune cells in the lymph nodes. Infected immune cells carry the virus into the bloodstream and infect cells throughout the body. Epithelial cells are especially targeted, causing the typical measles skin rash. Only killer T cells are able to finally destroy the virus. There's only one strain of measles, and it doesn't mutate. After infection, your body produces enough antibodies to prevent reinfection, and you should have lifetime immunity.

GUT VIRUSES

Measles, known for its rose-colored, flat rash, is a highly contagious viral infection that has largely been elIminated, including in the United States, but nonetheless remains a threat unless inoculation programs are maintained.

Enteric adenoviruses infect the intestines. They are spread when virus-contaminated water, food, or feces is ingested, and they are most prevalent where unsanitary conditions exist. Millions of children die every year from adenovirus-induced diarrhea.

Enteric adenoviruses have stronger protein coatings that enable them to withstand acids in the digestive tract as they head toward the intestines. These acids eat partway through the coat, and the virus's genetic material is free to infect cells. An adenovirus's double-stranded DNA is injected into a cell's nucleus. Viral proteins trigger viral DNA replication. In two days, one infected cell can produce 100,000 adenoviruses.

The slow but sure strategy of adenovirus replication might make it vulnerable to immune attack. But the virus is prepared and armed. The adenovirus contains proteins that prevent the death of infected and neighboring cells. So cell death does not trigger the immune system. Adenovirus proteins prevent the infected cell from displaying viral material on its surface. So killer T cells are not alerted to the infection. Another viral protein prevents attack by natural killer cells. Only after the virus has spread throughout the intestines are these immune cells finally able to combat it.

HEPATITIS: FROM POINT A TO B

The hepatitis A virus is also spread by contaminated food, water, and waste. Like the adenovirus, it enters the body orally. The single existing strain of hepatitis A targets liver cells. The well-armored, acid-resistant virus travels the digestive tract to the intestines. Here the virus infects cells and reproduces much like a rhinovirus—with one important difference. Hepatitis A rarely kills infected cells, unlike, say, a cold virus.

In the intestines, hepatitis A produces a limited infection that is easily neutralized by the immune system's B cells. But the

B cells carry it from the intestines to the liver for disposal. A weak intestinal virus becomes a powerful disease agent. Infected liver cells make countless copies of hepatitis A's single-stranded RNA before an immune response in the liver finally finishes them off. Meanwhile, the new viruses move from the liver to the bile ducts, back into the intestines, then out of the body with feces. The virus spreads so effectively because it remains viable for weeks in dried feces.

Hepatitis B also infects liver cells. Its double-stranded DNA is replicated in the infected cell's nucleus. Its replication strategy is truly bizarre, involving production of RNA, which makes a "backward" copy of DNA, which is then used to make "right-side-up" copies of DNA. While all this complicated copying is going on, viral coatings are being constructed out of cell proteins. Some coatings form around and enclose a copy of the virus's DNA. Other coatings form around—nothing! In fact, about 1,000 empty "decoy" viral envelopes exit the cell for every DNA-filled envelope. When B cells are finally activated, they are so busy binding to empty virus envelopes that lots of DNA-filled envelopes escape. And because hepatitis B doesn't kill infected cells, neither cell death nor interferon production alerts other parts of the immune system.

Hepatitis B is mostly passed from mother to child in the womb or in milk. It can also be spread by direct blood-to-blood contact. Hepatitis B can cause either acute or chronic infection. An acute infection is eventually eradicated when killer T cells destroy infected liver cells. Though the viral infection is gone, lifelong liver damage may result. About 90 percent of infants born with the virus live with a chronic, symptomless hepatitis B infection. Infected females will pass hepatitis B on to their children.

Shown magnified here are the characteristic spherical "Dane particles" of the hepatitis B virus. Untreated carriers often have no symptoms but may experience acute and chronic liver problems.

Hepatitis C always causes a chronic, long-term infection. It too attacks and damages the liver. Hepatitis C was first identified in 1989, so little is known about it. Yet it infects about 170 million people worldwide. It's transmitted from mother to child or through blood-to-blood contact. Hepatitis C binds to macrophages. It also attaches to lipoproteins (fat-protein complexes) in the blood. Since every body cell needs lipoproteins, all cells have receptors for it. Yet the virus "prefers" to bind to liver cells. Infected liver cells produce up to one trillion viruses daily!

The error rate in copying hepatitis C's genes is very large. Its constant mutations drive the immune system crazy. After the initial infection, antibodies and killer T cells recognize and conquer the virus. Just when the enemy seems to be wiped out, one or more mutant strains of hepatitis C virus emerge and attack. The immune system must start from scratch to fight them. This cat-and-mouse game occurs in six-week cycles. The virus is careful not to mutate too rapidly and risk killing its host. Nor does it mutate too slowly and risk being demolished by the immune system. Slow and steady mutation maintains an active and chronic infection.

Hepatitis C is spread to children mostly during childbirth. Intravenous drug users who share needles may transmit the infection in blood, as may blood transfusions. In most cases, people with chronic hepatitis C infections suffer no symptoms for decades. Eventually, continuous cycles of infection cause cirrhosis of the liver, which can be fatal.

THE 1918 FLU PANDEMIC

An epidemic is a locally intense outbreak of infection. A pandemic is a worldwide outbreak. In 1918, a pandemic of influenza A infected half the world's population. Twenty million people died, with most deaths among teenagers and young adults.

Every winter produces some influenza A outbreak. Each time, influenza A produces two or three minor mutations in its genes. Accumulation of small mutations is called antigenic drift, in which the virus slowly "drifts away" from its original genetic makeup. Antigenic shift, on the other hand, is a

(continued on the next page)

(continued from the previous page)

sudden and dramatic alteration of viral genes. This mutation has a devastating effect on host populations. Influenza A pandemics occur when antigenic shift gives rise to a new and highly virulent form of the virus.

In 1918, those killed outright by the flu virus died within two days of infection. Most others died within one or two weeks, not from the virus but from bacterial infections, especially pneumonia, that overcame the victims' weakened immune systems.

Influenza A pandemics occur every ten to forty years. The last occurred in 1968. It's not known what triggers an antigenic shift in influenza A.

HERPES: A CHRONIC, LIFELONG PROBLEM

There are several types of herpes virus. All produce lifelong, chronic infection. Herpes viruses are transmitted by physical contact and are often transmitted sexually.

Herpes simplex virus (HSV) produces a chronic infection by keeping a low profile in the body after initial infection. HSV invades epithelial cells around the skin and mucous membranes. After binding to a cell receptor, the virus fuses with the cell membrane. The virus's double-stranded DNA is injected into the cell and heads for the nucleus, where it's copied. HSV uses its proteins to take over all cellular processes. This allows the virus to replicate unhindered, killing infected cells. HSV's proteins are also employed in immune system evasion. Some HSV proteins bind with antibodies, rendering them useless. Even killer T cells are thwarted by HSV proteins. By the time the epithelial infection is defeated, the virus has created an escape route: a cold sore. Cold sores contain thousands of viruses, ready to spread to new hosts through direct contact or through saliva.

Infection of epithelial cells is only half the HSV story. A virus spread through physical contact must remain in the body to be transmitted to others. So after leaving the epithelial cells, some HSV migrates to nearby sensory nerve cells. HSV cannot reproduce in nerve cells. But it can hide in them. Once HSV is inside nerve cells, the immune system is unaware of it. This hidden infection lasts a lifetime. Occasionally, some HSV awakes, leaves the nerve cells, and re-infects epithelial cells, causing a painful skin disease.

CHICKENPOX

Chickenpox is a common childhood disease caused by the herpes varicella zoster virus (VZV). The first time you get VZV, it always causes chickenpox. Chickenpox is spread by contact with its virus-filled skin blisters. B cells destroy chickenpox and produce antibodies to ensure that you never get it again. However, like HSV, VZV hides in nerve cells. VZV may remain dormant in nerve cells for decades or, if you're lucky, forever. But sometimes,

VZV reawakens. When it does, it always shows up as shingles, a painful skin disorder. Shingles blisters are chock-full of VZV, and contact with them spreads the virus.

LATENT AND REACTIVATING VIRUSES

Persistent viruses are believed to be very ancient and to have spread to humans from nonhuman hosts. To be persistent, viruses need a latent (hidden and inactive) period, and so they must take up residence in long-lived cells. Nerve cells are perfect, for they generally don't die or even age.

Reactivation of latent viruses is not fully understood. Studies have shown that stress to the body may trigger latent viruses, like herpes, to wake up, replicate, and cause an active infection. Among the factors that trigger latent herpes reactivation are psychological or physical stress, sex, fevers and colds, or exposure to ultraviolet light. These factors sometimes compromise or weaken the immune system. It's possible that persistent viruses are "aware" of the state of the immune system in an infected host. When they "sense" a weakness, viruses leave nerve cells for target cells, where they replicate and cause a new round of infection.

HPV

One virus sometimes confused with herpes among sufferers is the human papillomavirus (HPV), probably because it produces skin warts. Each of the hundred or so HPVs specializes in infecting basal cells (in the innermost part of the skin) in a particular part of the body. Each has protein receptors to match those on the target basal cells. The virus's double-stranded DNA is replicated in the infected cell's nucleus. At some stage, HPV replicates wildly in basal cells, eventually pushing masses of infected cells to the skin surface, producing a wart. Physical contact spreads the virus to a new host.

Skin cells are always being replaced, and thus basal cells are always reproducing. This makes them a great candidate for targeting by viruses producing chronic infections. HPV also attacks the immune system by creating proteins that prevent adjacent cells from committing suicide. HPV also doesn't produce double-stranded RNA during replication, so infected cells don't produce interferon. Altogether, these characteristics of HPV make it stick around for good. While killer T cells take care of some HPV cells, "sleeper" viruses hiding out in basal cells lie in wait to infect the host again.

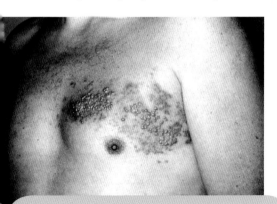

These are lesions on the skin of someone suffering from herpes zoster, commonly known as shingles. They can arise years after a person suffered from chickenpox.

23

CHAPTER 3

THE DANGERS OF RETROVIRUSES

Whereas many viruses carry genetic material as DNA, a retrovirus carries its genetic material as RNA. Retroviruses violate what was thought to be a fundamental law of biology: that DNA forms RNA and not vice versa. But retroviral RNA is capable of working "backward" and creating viral DNA, which then creates more viral RNA to build more viruses inside the host cell.

Retroviruses generally produce no fancy proteins to control cell reproduction or to "outsmart" the immune system. They don't have to. When a retrovirus's DNA is safely tucked away inside the cell, the virus is home free. It attracts no attention from the immune system. The cell's normal reproduction ensures the persistence of the retrovirus.

HTLV-1

HTLV-1 (human T-cell lymphotropic virus, type 1) was the first retrovirus discovered, in 1980. HTLV-1 attaches to and infects helper T cells via an unknown receptor on the cell surface. It replicates in helper T cells. After its DNA is produced, a viral enzyme called integrase cuts the cell's DNA and inserts the viral DNA into the cell's genes. Every time the infected helper T cell reproduces, its daughter cells and all their descendants contain the virus's genes. Replication of HTLV-1 is thus rather slow, depending as it does on cell division. HTLV-1 doesn't kill the infected cells it relies on to reproduce it. Most of the time, HTLV-1 lays low. Infected people carry it for life, but about 95 percent never suffer from an HTLV1-induced disease.

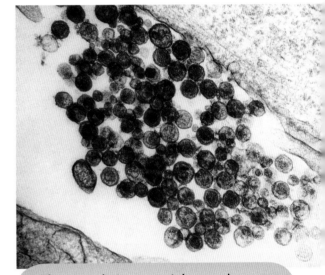

These red virus particles are known as human T- cell lymphotropic virus 1 (HTLV-1). It was the first retrovirus to be isolated in humans. The virus causes many ailments, including adult T-cell leukemia.

Decades after infection, about 5 percent of infected people will develop cancer. HTLV-1 is associated with adult T-cell leukemia. Causing a disease that kills its host (along with the virus) is an unintended result of infection. Scientists believe that leukemia arises because the viral DNA eventually causes mutations in the helper T cell's own genes. HTLV-1 is spread through blood, so intravenous drug users may transmit it. It can also be spread through semen during sex. Women with HTLV-1 in their blood may pass it to infants through breast milk.

HIV/AIDS

HIV (human immunodeficiency virus), another retrovirus, was first identified in 1983. It was soon shown to cause AIDS (acquired immunodeficiency syndrome), a devastating and deadly condition that destroys the immune system.

HIV infects immune system cells with certain surface receptors. Its primary targets are helper T cells and macrophages. HIV's RNA enters the host cell's genes in typical retrovirus fashion. However, HIV also has a protein that boosts HIV's infection rate. When an infected cell begins proliferating, this protein induces the cell to produce a thousand times more HIV genes than cell genes. The new viruses, many of them mutants, bud from the cell, enter the blood, and seek more cells to infect.

Initially, HIV infects macrophages and other cells, but it doesn't kill them. At this early stage, there are enough helper T cells to activate killer T cells, which control the HIV infection. Initial infection usually causes flulike symptoms, which disappear in a few weeks. Then HIV begins its seven- to ten-year-long period of latency.

Though the infection seems to be under control during latency, wave after wave of macrophages and other cells

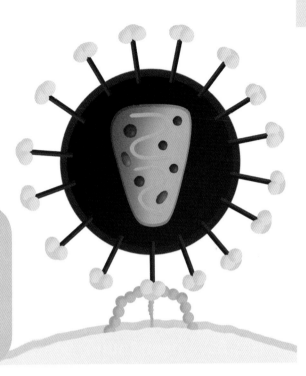

In this HIV virus model, envelope proteins (dark blue spokes with yellow ends) attach to the host cell. Within are the identical strands of RNA (light blue) and the transcriptase (dark blue circles) that converts RNA to DNA.

become infected with HIV. The immune system produces helper T cells, which mobilize killer T cells to fight the virus. This battle against HIV is continuous and ferocious. Yet the HIV-infected person feels perfectly healthy. There are no outward signs of infection, though HIV is present in blood and other body fluids. It is during latency that HIV is most often spread by unaware carriers.

HIV completely disrupts and turns the immune system against itself. At some point during the long latency, HIV mutates in such a way that infected cells are able to pass the virus on to helper T cells in the lymph nodes. HIV kills the helper T cells it infects. Helper T cells are crucial to the immune system. Without them, B cells and killer T cells are not generated.

CANCER AND VIRUSES

Scientists estimate that 10 to 20 percent of cancers involve viruses. In 1961, British physician Dennis Burkitt, while working in Africa, noticed that a deadly childhood tumor occurred only in specific climatic conditions. He concluded that this cancer was caused by a virus carried by an insect native to this climate. In 1964, British virologist Anthony Epstein identified this cancer-causing virus, naming it Epstein-Barr virus (EBV). The cancer became known as Burkitt's lymphoma.

Since the discovery of EBV, five more cancer-inducing viruses have been found. Some forms of papilloma virus are linked to cervical cancer. Hepatitis B and C can cause liver cancer. Herpes virus 8, discovered in 1994, causes Kaposi's sarcoma.

Cancer arises through a multistep process, involving uncontrolled reproduction of cells. A virus that interferes with any step in cell reproduction might contribute to the onset of cancer. This may occur, for example, when viruses shut off cells' reproductive controls to get them to replicate viral genes or when viral proteins disable tumor suppressor genes.

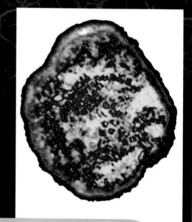

The Epstein-Barr virus (EBV), also called human herpes virus 4, can cause mononucleosis, or mono, which causes fatigue, fever, inflammation, swelling, and rashes and is highly contagious.

In the lymph nodes, HIV infects millions, then billions of helper T cells. The infected cells proliferate, each producing thousands of viruses, and then are killed. The lymph nodes become huge reservoirs of the virus. The lymph nodes become HIV factories where an unbelievable 100 billion new viruses are produced every day!

The desperate immune system daily cranks out billions of new helper T cells. But they, too, quickly become infected with mutant HIV. The more helper T cells the body produces, the worse the infection becomes. Instead of fighting the infection, these desperately needed immune system cells are themselves infected, produce more HIV, and are then killed by it. The result is a relentless downward spiral in which the supply of helper T cells dwindles to near nothing and mutant HIV overruns the immune system.

One microliter of healthy human blood contains about 1,200 T cells. A microliter of blood from a person completely beaten by HIV contains only 200 T cells. With so few helper T cells, the immune system is essentially destroyed. The infected person now has AIDS. During full-blown

An HIV rapid testing kit is pictured here in a mobile testing vehicle in Paris, France. Quicker detection of the HIV virus in recent years has helped save lives.

VIRUSES

AIDS, up to 2 billion immune system cells are killed in the body every day.

Opportunistic infections—infections that healthy immune systems easily defeat—can often overwhelm AIDS sufferers. In fact, these are often the direct cause of death for those who catch HIV. One of the first opportunistic infections to plague AIDS patients is herpes virus 8, the cause of a type of skin cancer called Kaposi's sarcoma.

The body can be overcome by a host of different fungal, bacterial, and viral infections, many which are otherwise rare for healthy individuals. African AIDS sufferers are particularly affected by wasting disease, for example. Other common ailments include untreatable strains of pneumonia or tuberculosis. Brain infections causing memory loss, tremors, epilepsy, and even psychosis can occur, as well as bacterial infections that bring on neurological disorders. In general, HIV enables a whole host of horrific diseases and conditions.

CHAPTER 4

EMERGING VIRUSES AND TREATMENTS

Humans entering, occupying, and often destroying pre-viously uninhabited areas is one of the factors that has exposed human beings to new and fearsome viruses—many of which they have little or no immunity to. For example, loggers entering remote forests in Africa are likely to have had HIV transmitted to them by wild chimpanzees. Some even theorize that humans eating infected chimpanzee meat did the trick.

Rain forest destruction in particular has led to new viral infections. The infamous and lethal hemorrhagic viruses—Ebola and Marburg—emerged mainly from human intrusion into rain forests. Before, these viruses existed quietly and harm-lessly among species adapted to harbor them. The Ebola virus first appeared in humans in the remote forests of Zaire in 1976. Hemorrhagic viruses cause bleeding from all parts of the body. They are spread by physical contact, are highly infectious, and in humans, are nearly always fatal.

VIRUSES

Medical volunteers are covered head to toe in protective biosuits as they prepare to bury seven deceased victims of the Ebola virus outbreak of 2014 in Kenema, Sierra Leone.

Climate change arising from natural cycles and emissions of fossil fuels (oil, gas, coal) is also spreading new viruses. When the West Nile virus reached New York from Africa in 1999, experts believed that the city's cold winters would kill its mosquito carriers. But mosquitoes have survived several abnormally warm winters and have even spread farther north. Other insect-borne viruses, such as yellow fever and dengue fever, have also benefited from global temperatures rising. Their insect carriers have increased their range to regions that were once too cold for them.

BAD MEAT AND MAD COWS

In 1986, British cows became diseased. They staggered and trembled, then died. Mad cow disease, or BSE (bovine spongiform encephalopathy), was quickly traced to the practice of feeding cattle the ground-up body parts from slaughtered cows. Turning vegetarian cows into cannibals by feeding them cheap dead-cow protein saved the meat industry lots of money in feed costs. But it also allowed BSE to spread wildly. By the late 1990s, millions of British cows and sheep had been slaughtered to prevent the spread of BSE. By that time, several people had contracted and died from a human form of BSE, called Creutzfeldt-Jakob disease (CJD). Like BSE, CJD causes spongelike holes in the brain and is always fatal.

Evidence indicates that BSE and CJD are caused not by a virus but by infectious versions of normal brain proteins. The normal protein can be broken down and discarded by enzymes. But somehow prions change their form and become "unbreakable." Enzymes can't remove them. Prions accumulate in the brain, where they continuously convert normal proteins into deadly prions. Prions also do not elicit an immune response in the body. Prion infection causes no inflammation, and it doesn't activate antibodies or killer T cells.

VIRUSES

These new viruses are not really new, but old viruses adapted to nonhuman hosts in tropical climates. These viruses have jumped to humans because of our intrusion into uninhabited areas and because of our altering of the world climate.

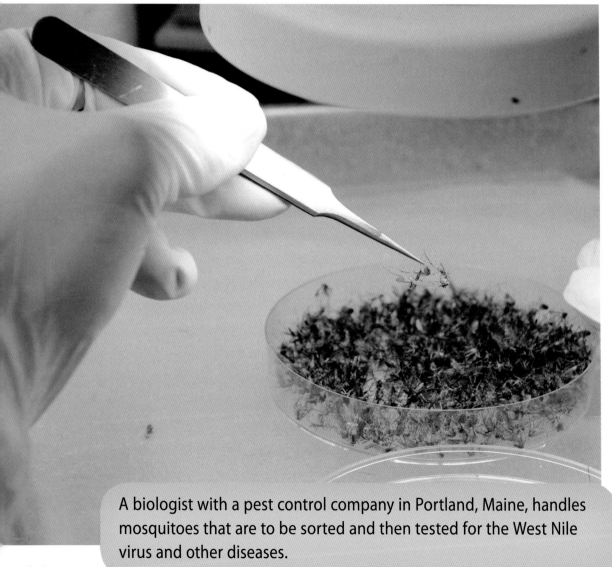

A biologist with a pest control company in Portland, Maine, handles mosquitoes that are to be sorted and then tested for the West Nile virus and other diseases.

VACCINATIONS AND TREATMENTS

A vaccine is a virus preparation intended to be benign to the recipient but sufficiently potent to initiate an immune response when injected into the body. In the course of fighting the limited infection, the immune system produces antibodies that stay in the body and safeguard against future infection.

Some noninfectious vaccines are made from dead viruses. The defunct viruses generate memory immune cells but generally don't cause infection. Some polio vaccine is made this way. Another strategy is to make viruses out of pieces of viral proteins or even "naked" pieces of viral DNA. These vaccines stimulate the immune system to produce antibodies. Because they're incomplete parts of viruses, an infection cannot occur. This type of vaccine is effective against hepatitis B. Attenuated or weakened viruses are grown in the tissues of nonhuman animals. When injected into humans as vaccine, the weakened virus is unable to cause infection, but it does induce antibody production.

Attenuated vaccines immunize against mumps, measles, and rubella (German measles), and have the advantage of producing lifelong immunity, something that noninfectious vaccines cannot guarantee. Finally, there are new vaccines whose DNA induces production of both memory B cells and killer T cells. The vaccine is made from DNA that codes for only a few viral proteins, so it cannot cause infection.

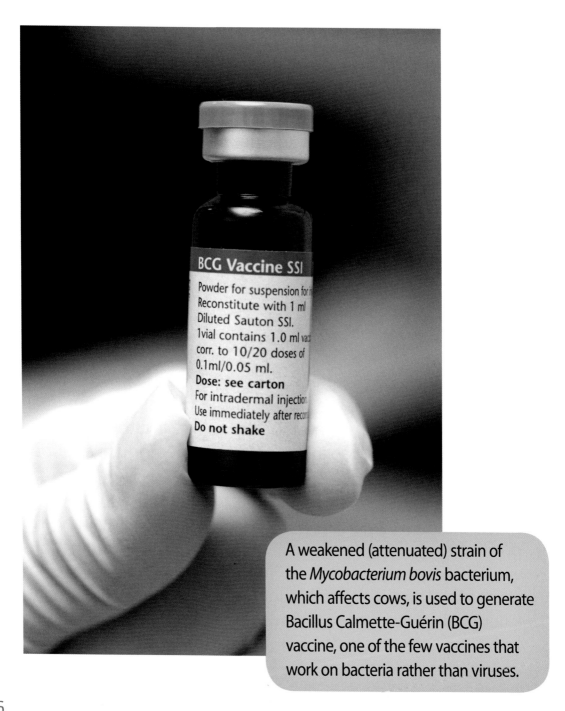

A weakened (attenuated) strain of the *Mycobacterium bovis* bacterium, which affects cows, is used to generate Bacillus Calmette-Guérin (BCG) vaccine, one of the few vaccines that work on bacteria rather than viruses.

ERADICATING SMALLPOX

Smallpox is a horrible viral disease that used to kill millions of people. In 1796, Dr. Edward Jenner noticed that milkmaids who got cowpox blisters from milking cows never got smallpox. He concluded that the harmless cowpox blisters somehow made the milkmaids immune to smallpox. Jenner inoculated a young boy with cowpox taken from a blister on a milkmaid's hand. Weeks later, he injected the boy with active smallpox. The boy did not contract smallpox; he was now immune to it. Jenner had discovered and successfully used the first antiviral vaccine. By 1976, the World Health Organization's worldwide vaccination campaign eradicated smallpox completely.

Sometimes vaccines are used to treat, not prevent, viral infection. Rabies vaccine is a case in point. Rabies reproduces slowly in the body and usually takes a rather long time to reach its destination in the brain. A vaccine administered after infection usually gives the immune system enough time to mobilize and destroy the infection.

VIRUSES

Very high inoculation rates are one way for public health authorities and communities to ensure that viral infections do not arise, or spread very widely if they do. Here, a doctor gives a teen girl a booster shot.

Aside from vaccines, antiviral drugs aim to disrupt viruses during one particular stage of infection: during entry, uncoating, gene replication, or exit from a cell. To date, no drug can disrupt a virus's entry into a cell.

One new drug can disrupt the uncoating of the influenza A virus. The drug interferes with a viral protein that "unzips" the virus's coat, so viral genes cannot be released into the cell. Though promising, the drug cannot counter influenza A's rapid mutation rate, which alters the targeted viral protein.

AZT, the drug used to treat AIDS, interferes with the replication of the retrovirus. Enzymes in the cell convert AZT into a protein that attaches to viral DNA, preventing the DNA from assembling and stopping replication.

GLOSSARY

CYTOPLASM The clear liquid substance inside cells but outside the nucleus that contains organelles.

DNA (DEOXYRIBONUCLEIC ACID) The hereditary material found in cells.

ENTERIC ADENOVIRUS An often fatal intestinal virus that causes diarrhea.

ENZYME A protein that causes biochemical reactions to occur in cells.

GENE A unit of heredity, made of chemicals (DNA) that carry the instructions for passing on traits from parents to offspring during reproduction.

HEMORRHAGIC VIRUS A virus that causes fever and hemorrhaging (bleeding), such as the Ebola virus.

HOST An organism that is invaded by and whose life functions support a virus or other parasite.

INFLAMMATION A condition in which part of the human body reacts negatively to infection, becoming inflamed, swollen, red, and hot, or experiencing pain.

INOCULATION Building up the immune system's resistance to a potential future infection by introducing an altered, weakened, or related (yet not as potent) infection into a patient.

INTERFERON A signaling or alarm protein that interferes with viral replication in infected cells.

MACROPHAGE One of the cells in the human immune systems that engulfs foreign particles or cells, acting as a scavenger or "garbage collector" within the body.

VIRUSES

NUCLEUS A membrane-covered part of a cell that contains DNA.

PANDEMIC A huge outbreak of infection, often spanning multiple continents or even the whole world.

PARASITE A virus or an organism that lives on or in another organism and that gets food or protection from the host, which is often harmed.

PROTEIN A primary part of living things, containing substances consisting mainly of nitrogen and carbon; the "building blocks" of organisms.

RECEPTOR A part of the surface of a cell that is specialized for receiving a particular material, which attaches to the receptor.

RETROVIRUS A virus that carries its genetic material as RNA, not DNA.

RNA (RIBONUCLEIC ACID) A substance found mainly in the cytoplasm that carries out DNA's instructions for making vital cell proteins.

FOR MORE INFORMATION

Association of Medical Microbiology and Infectious Disease Canada (AMMI)
192 Bank Street
Ottawa K2P 1W8
Canada
(613) 260-3233
info@ammi.ca
Website: http://www.ammi.ca
The Association of Medical Microbiology and Infectious Disease Canada (AMMI) promotes the prevention, diagnosis, and treatment of human infectious diseases through its involvement in education, research, clinical practice, and patient advocacy.

Canadian Foundation for Infectious Diseases
The Hospital for Sick Children
c/o Dr. Susan Richardson
Room 3654 Atrium
555 University Avenue
Toronto, ON M5G 1X8
Canada
(416) 813-5990
cfid@researchid.com
Website: http://www.researchid.com
The Canadian Foundation for Infectious Diseases (CFID) seeks solutions to better understand, diagnose, control, and treat existing and emerging infections that threaten public health.

VIRUSES

Centers for Disease Control and Prevention (CDC)
1600 Clifton Road
Atlanta, GA 30333
Website: http://www.cdc.gov
The CDC is the primary United States government agency in
charge of tracking, treating, and preventing public health
threats, including infectious diseases.

Doctors Without Borders/Médecins Sans Frontières
333 7th Avenue
New York, NY 10001
(212) 679-6800
Website: http://www.doctorswithoutborders.org
Doctors Without Borders (founded originally by French doctors in 1970 as Médecins Sans Frontières) is an international
humanitarian organization dedicated to providing medical aid
to civilians in war zones and citizens of developing nations fac-
ing disease.

National Institutes of Health (NIH)
9000 Rockville Pike
Bethesda, MD 20892
(301) 496-4000
NIHinfo@od.nih.gov
Website: http://www.nih.gov
The National Institutes of Health (NIH) is a research facility in the
Washington, DC, area that is the primary agency of the United
States government in charge of biomedical and health-related
research.

The World Health Organization (WHO)
Avenue Appia 20
1211 Geneva 27
Switzerland
Website: http://www.who.int/en
The World Health Organization is the specialized agency of the United Nations that is primarily concerned with international public health.

WEBSITES

Because of the changing nature of Internet links, Rosen Publishing has developed an online list of websites related to the subject of this book. This site is updated regularly. Please use this link to access the list:

http://www.rosenlinks.com/GDCO/virus

FOR FURTHER READING

Crawford, Dorothy H. *Viruses: A Very Short Introduction*. New York, NY: Oxford University Press, 2011.

Crawford, Dorothy H. *Virus Hunt: The Search for the Origin of HIV/AIDS*. New York, NY: Oxford University Press, 2013.

Facklam, Howard. *Viruses*. New York, NY: Twenty-First Century Books, 1995.

Goldsmith, Connie. *The Ebola Epidemic: The Fight, The Future*. Minneapolis, MN: Twenty-First Century Books, 2016.

Markovics, Joyce L. *Tiny Invaders!: Deadly Microorganisms* (Nature's Invaders) Mankato, MN: Capstone Press, 2013.

Quammen, David. *Ebola: The Natural and Human History of a Deadly Virus*. New York, NY: W. W. Norton, 2014.

Quammen, David. *Spillover: Animal Infections and the Next Human Pandemic*. New York, NY: W. W. Norton, 2013.

Rodriguez, A. M. *Edward Jenner: Conqueror of Smallpox* (Great Minds of Science). Berkeley Heights, NJ: Enslow Publishers, 2006.

Roy, Jonathan. *Smallpox Zero: An Illustrated History of Smallpox and Its Eradication*. Atlanta, GA: Emory Global Health Institute, 2010.

Smith, Linda Wasmer. *Louis Pasteur: Genius Disease Fighter* (Genius Scientists and Their Genius Ideas). New York, NY: Enslow Publishing, 2015.

Whiteside, Alan. *HIV/AIDS: A Very Short Introduction* (Very Short Introductions). New York, NY: Oxford University Press, 2008.

Willett, Edward. *Infectious Disease Specialists: Hunting Down Disease* (Extreme Science Careers). New York, NY: Enslow Publishing, 2015.

Williams, Gareth. *Angel of Death: The Story of Smallpox*. New York, NY: Palgrave Macmillian, 2010.

Zimmer, Carl. *A Planet of Viruses: Second Edition*. Chicago, IL: University of Chicago Press, 2015.

BIBLIOGRAPHY

BBC News. "Ebola: Mapping the Outbreak." December 24, 2015. Retrieved January 8, 2016 (http://www.bbc.com/news/world-africa-28755033).

CDC. "Cases of Ebola Diagnosed in the United States." Retrieved January 2016 (http://www.cdc.gov/vhf/ebola/outbreaks/2014-west-africa/united-states-imported-case.html).

Crawford, Dorothy H. *The Invisible Enemy: A Natural History of Viruses.* Oxford, England: Oxford University Press, 2000.

Crawford, Dorothy H. *Viruses: A Very Short Introduction.* New York, NY: Oxford University Press, 2011.

Sompayrac, Lauren. *How Pathogenic Viruses Work.* London, England: Jones & Bartlett Publishers, 2002.

Zimmer, Carl. *A Planet of Viruses: Second Edition.* Chicago, IL: University of Chicago Press, 2015.

INDEX

ABOUT THE AUTHORS

Margaux Baum is a young adult nonfiction author from Queens, New York. She has written numerous books for Rosen Publishing covering disease prevention, drug addiction, and science.

Natalie Goldstein has been a writer of science and educational materials for more than two decades. She has written extensively about environmental, life, and the physical sciences. Among her books are *Earth Almanac*, *Rebuilding Prairies and Forests*, and *The Nature of the Atom*. She has worked for the Nature Conservancy, the Hudson River Foundation, the World Wildlife Fund, and the Audubon Society. A member of the National Association of Science Writers and the Society of Environmental Journalists, Ms. Goldstein holds master's degrees in environmental science and education.

PHOTO CREDITS

Designer: Brian Garvey; Photo researcher: Philip Wolny